HOORAY for CATS

COMPILED BY
WELLERAN
POLTARNEES

HOORAY
for CATS

LAUGHING ELEPHANT · MMIX

LAUGHING ELEPHANT

WWW.LAUGHINGELEPHANT.COM

Introduction

No other animal has managed to get itself tangled up in as much legend, myth, symbolism, religion, history, and human affairs as the cat. From the time it first appeared upon the scene some four thousand years ago, it has played its part in almost every age. And indeed, one of the chief and yet unsolved mysteries connected with this animal is that before the earliest Egyptian dynasties and wall decorations, there is no record of this animal at all, neither in cave art or kitchen middens. It is as though it suddenly appeared on earth, neatly packaged and with all its qualities practically as we know it today.

PAUL GALLICO

Perhaps one reason we are fascinated by cats, is because such a small animal can contain so much independence, dignity and freedom of spirit. Unlike the dog, the cat's personality is never bet on a human's. He demands acceptance on his own terms as the wildest of tame animals and the tamest of wild ones.

There are other ties which cats put on our affections. We enjoy their intelligence and grace; and we feel a strange sense of companionship and consolation in their presence. But these are ideas we can understand by words. At bottom cats are like music. The reasons for their appeal to us can never be expressed too clearly.

LLOYD ALEXANDER

There are Tabbies and Tortoiseshell, Black Cats and White,

All happy and purring from morning till night

And though they do mischief sometimes, which is wrong,

They're so pretty, you cannot be cross with them long.

NURSERY RHYME

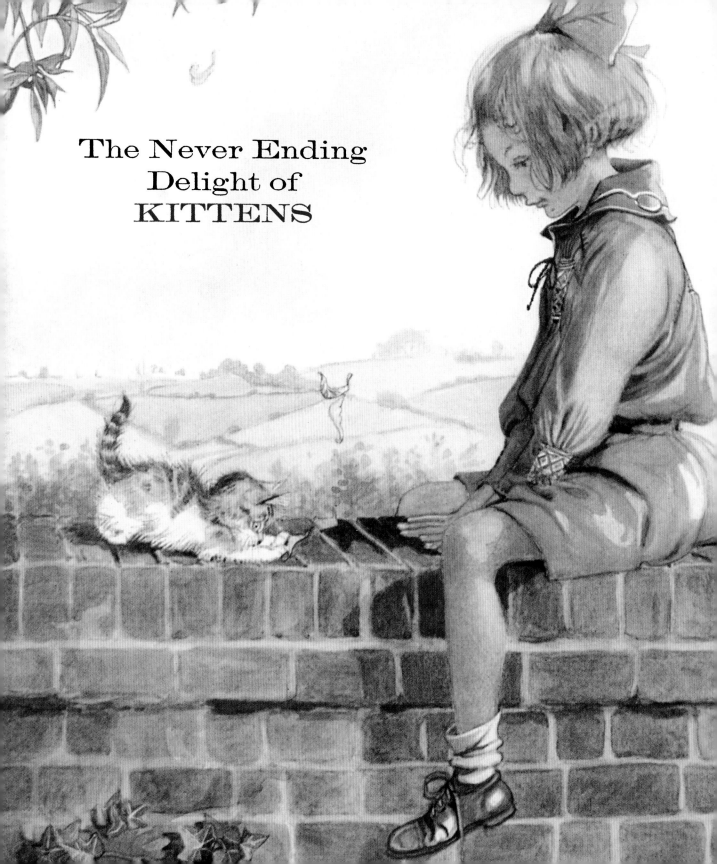

The Never Ending
Delight of
KITTENS

A kitten is so flexible that she is almost double; the hind parts are equivalent to another kitten with which the forepart plays. She does not discover that her tail belongs to her until you tread upon it.

HENRY DAVID THOREAU

What is prettier or more fascinating than a kitten, or better still, two kittens, at play? It calls a smile of amusement and admiration to the gravest countenance, to watch the grotesque movements, the marvelous activity, the exquisite gracefulness, of these sportive little creatures.

SARAH J. EDDY

An ordinary kitten will ask more questions than any five-year-old boy. He is the most catechismal of animals, with the possible exception of the monkey. Curiosity, indeed, is a predominant cat trait and a cat's first duty on entering a new domain is to explore every square inch of it. He not only examines every corner of the house he lives in but investigates the country for miles around. All right then: one morning—for this present usually arrives in the night—in some corner half a dozen kitten will be squeaking; the cat will reply to them with her sweet cooing, a note which she reserves only for them; it is not a note, but a whole chord in harmonic third and fifth, very similar to the chord on a mouth-organ. She would be ready to melt with her display of motherhood; every movement will be infinitely protective and soft; her ruffled body, patiently curved back, and her small tender paws will embrace the swarming kittens in one maternal all: see, we are one body. Only for a wink will she leave her nest, to return at a trot from the distance calling and cooing; it will be perfect fanaticism of motherhood.

KAREL ĈAPEK

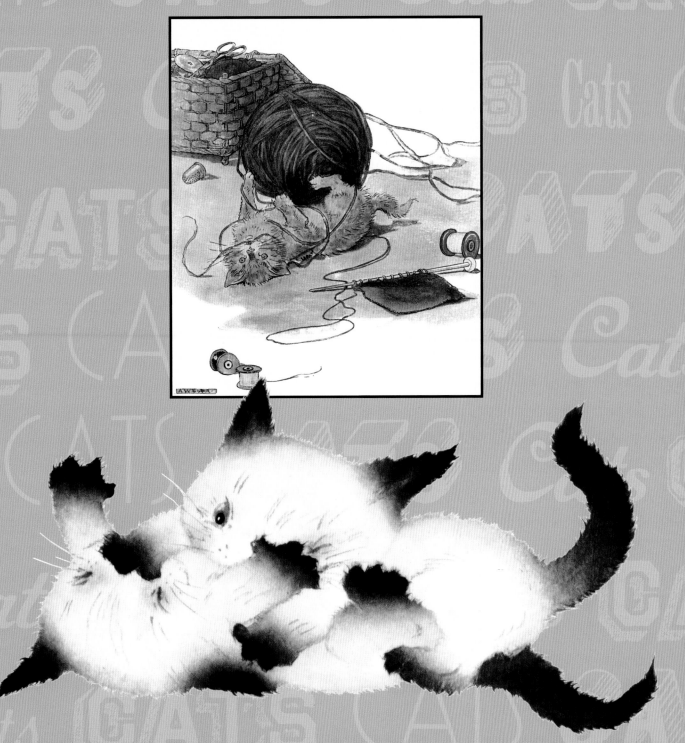

Everything that moves serves to amuse them. They are convinced that Nature is occupied solely with their diversion; they do not conceive of any other cause for motion; and when by our movements we incite them to graceful tumbling, may it not be that they take us merely for pantomimists, all of whose actions are jokes?

MONCRIFF

We realize this with kittens; we see that the greater part of their life, of the sights and sounds of it, is the material of a drama half consciously played; they are determined to make mysteries, and as a child will seize upon the passing light or shadow to help him to transform some well-known object into the semblance of a living creature, so you may see the kitten reach a paw again and again to touch a reflection on a polished floor, or conjure the shadows of evening into the forms of enemies.

MARGARET BENSON

I have a kitten, my dear, the drollest of all creatures that ever wore a cat's skin. Her gambols are not to be described, and would be incredible, if they could. She tumbles head over heels several times together. She lays her cheek to the ground, and humps her back at you with an air of most supreme disdain. From this posture she rises to dance on her hind feet, an exercise which she performs with all the grace imaginable; and she closes these various exhibitions with a loud smack of her lips, which, for want of a greater propriety of expression, we call spitting.

WILLIAM COWPER

He is entirely self-reliant. He lives in homes because he chooses to do so, and as long as the surroundings and the people suit him, but he lives there on his own terms, and never sacrifices his own comfort or his own well-being for the sake of the stupid folk with whom, he comes in contact. Thus he is the most satisfactory of friends.

CARL VAN VECHTEN

He would lie or sit with his whiskers to the North before noonday, and due South afterwards. In general his manners were perfection. But occasionally when she called him, his face would appear to knot itself into a frown— at any rate to assume a low sullen look, as if he expostulated "Why must you be interrupting me, Madam, when I am thinking of something else?"

WALTER DE LA MARE

KITTENS

See the Kitten on the Wall,
Sporting with the leaves that fall,
Wither'd leaves, one, two, and three,
From the lofty Elder-tree!
Through the calm and frosty air
Of this morning bright and fair,
Eddying round and round they sink
Softly, slowly: one might think,
From the motions that are made,
Every little leaf convey'd
Sylph or Faery hither tending,
To this lower world descending,
Each invisible and mute,
In his wavering parachute.
--But the Kitten, how she starts,
Crouches, stretches, paws, and darts;
First at one and then it's fellow
Just as light and just as yellow;
There are many now--now one--
Now they stop; and there are none--
What intenseness of desire
In her upward eye of fire!

With a tiger-leap half way
Now she meets the coming prey,
Lets it go as fast, and then
Has it in her power again:
Now she works with three or four,
Like an Indian Conjuror;
Quick as he in feats of art,
Far beyond in joy of heart.
Were her antics play'd in the eye
Of a thousand Standers-by,
Clapping hands with shout and stare,
What would little Tabby care
For the plaudits of the Crowd?

WILLIAM WORDSWORTH

…Now, wheeling round, with bootless skill,
Thy bo-peep tail provokes thee still,
As oft beyond thy curving side
Its jetty tip is seen to glide;
Till, from thy centre starting far,
Thou sidelong rear'st, with rump in air …

Doth power in measured verses dwell,
All thy vagaries wild to tell?
Ah, no! the start, the jet, the bound,
The giddy scamper round and round,
With leap, and jerk, and high curvet,
And many a whirling somerset …

JOANNA BAILLIE

A kitten is in the animal world what a
rosebud is in the garden.

ROBERT SOUTHEY

Their Beautiful
DESIGN

His personal appearance had much to do with this, for he was of royal mould, and had an air of high breeding. He was large, but he had nothing of the fat grossness of the celebrated Angora family; though powerful, he was exquisitely proportioned, and as graceful in every movement as a young leopard. When he stood up to open a door—he opened all the doors with old-fashioned latches—he was portentously tall, and when stretched on the rug before the fire he seemed too long for this world—as indeed he was. His coat was the finest and softest I have ever seen, a shade of quiet Maltese; and from his throat downward, underneath, to the white tips of his feet, he wore the whitest and most delicate ermine; and no person was ever more fastidiously neat. In his finely formed head you saw something of his aristocratic character; the ears were small and cleanly cut, there was a tinge of pink in the nostrils, his face was handsome, and the expression of his countenance exceedingly intelligent—I should call it even a sweet expression if the term were not inconsistent with his look of alertness and sagacity.

CHARLES DUDLEY WARNER

Silently licking his gold-white paw,
Oh gorgeous Celestino, for
God made lovely things, yet
Our lovely cat surpasses them all;
The gold, the iron, the waterfall,
The nut, the peach, apple, granite
Are lovely things to look at yet
Our lovely cat surpasses them all.

JOHN GITTINGS

What a beautiful Pussy you are,
You are,
You are!
What a beautiful Pussy you are!

EDWARD LEAR

The beauty of the cat is very deceptive, for under the grace of the furry exterior lie concealed steel-like muscles. Now the artist who indicates the grace and softness usually misses the strength and the artist who seizes the strength usually does so at the expense of other qualities.

CARL VAN VECHTEN

The most aesthetic souls of all time have cherished the cat, Baudelaire, Von Scheffel, Poe, De Musset, Henry Irving and a host of other lovers of the beautiful come to mind in this connection. The silky feline of padded footfall and mysterious wanderings has ever appealed to the imagination, just as she has ever appealed to the sense of domestic comfort.

MARY LEE

If a fish is the movement of water embodied, given shape, then cat is a diagram and pattern of subtle air.

DORIS LESSING

Nature's Masterpiece

LEONARDO DA VINCI

For God has blessed him in the variety of his movements.
For, he cannot fly, he is an excellent clamberer.
For his motions upon the face of the earth are more than other quadrupeds.
For he can tread to all the measures upon the musick.
For he can swim for life.
For he can creep.

CHRISTOPHER SMART

It begins, I should say, with the compactness of construction, composition, size, proportion, and general overall form. The domesticated cat is the tidiest of all animals. There is an almost divine neatness and economy about the animal. Completely packaged in fur with not a bald spot showing, rarely two specimens wholly alike, it often comes decorated with designs that Picasso might envy and always functionally streamlined for every activity; just another case of the practical made glamorous.

PAUL GALLICO

Two things are aesthetically perfect in the world—the clock and the cat.

ALAIN

The cat is the most beautiful and graceful of all domestic animals. His anatomy is precisely adapted to his needs; and although he takes only a hundredth part as much exercise as a dog, he is always in perfect condition.

WILLIAM LYON PHELPS

All their colors, all the ways they swirl and combine, as complex and satisfying in their infinite design and shifting colors as Oriental carpets.

PAUL SYMONDS

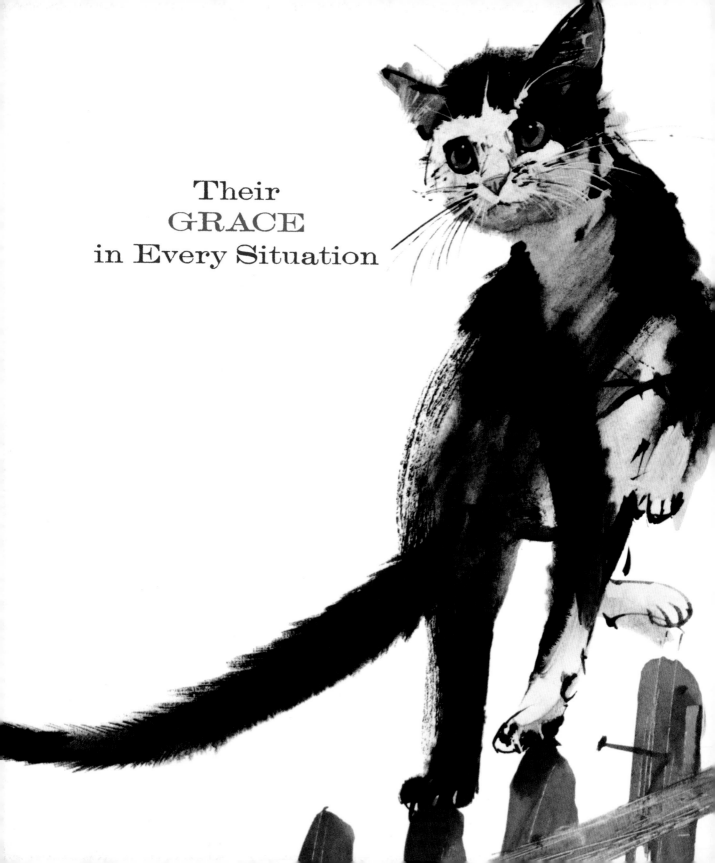

Their
GRACE
in Every Situation

TIRZAH GARWOOD

An attitude need not be static. A cat running is a flow of rhythm and coordination which, in a moment, can be turned to the most amusing burlesque when it decides to gallop and bring its padded feet down hard upon the floor. Or is there any lazier or more luxurious movement than the cat getting up and stretching? Always, always, is the eye diverted and the intellect of appreciation stimulated by movement. House Cat jumping, pouncing, playing, rolling, cruising; each of these has its moments of supreme delectation. Nothing the animal does is ungraceful.

PAUL GALLICO

Cats, no less liquid than their shadows,
Offer no angles to the wind,
They slip, diminished, neat through loopholes
Less than themselves; will not be pinned.

To rules or routes for journeys; counter
Attack with non-resistance; twist
Enticing through the curving fingers
And leave an angered, empty fist.

A.S.J. TESSIMOND

Now when the cat decides to take his repose, he not only lies down, he pours his body out on the floor like water. It is restful merely to behold him.

WILLIAM LYON PHELPS

How many times have I rested tired eyes on her graceful little body, curled up in a ball and wrapped round with her tail like a parcel; or stretched out luxuriously on my bed, one paw covering her face, the other curved gently inwards, as though clasping an invisible treasure. Asleep or awake, in rest, in motion, grave or gay, Agrippina is always beautiful; and it is better to be beautiful than to fetch and carry from the rising to the setting of the sun.

But when Agrippina has breakfasted and washed, and sits in the sunlight blinking at me with affectionate contempt, I feel soothed by her absolute and unqualified enjoyment. I know how full my day will be of things that I don't want particularly to do, and that are not particularly worth doing; but for her, time and the world hold only this brief moment of contentment. Slowly the eyes close, gently the little body is relaxed. Oh, you who strive to relieve your overwrought nerves and cultivate power through repose, watch the exquisite languor of a drowsy cat and despair of imitating such perfect and restful grace. There is a gradual yielding of every muscle to the soft persuasiveness of slumber: the flexible frame is curved into tender lines, the head nestles lower, the paws are tucked out of sight; no convulsive throb or start betrays a rebellious alertness; only a faint quiver of unconscious satisfaction, a faint heaving of the tawny sides, a faint gleam of the half-shut yellow eyes, and Agrippina is asleep. I look at her for one wistful moment and then turn resolutely to my work. It were ignoble to wish myself in her place; and yet how charming to be able to settle down to a nap sans peur et sans reproche at ten o'clock in the morning.

AGNES REPPLIER

When a cat aims at the top of a fence or the surface of a table, he usually succeeds at the first attempt, unlike the dog, who tries five or six times and continues to try after the impossibility of the attainment has been clearly demonstrated. The cat's economy of effort is as remarkable as his judgment of distance; you can not try to persuade him to try for any mark manifestly beyond his reach.

WILLIAM LYON PHELPS

Their Profound
DIGNITY

After eating, he retired to the living room, took his position under the harp, or on top of the piano, and gave out word that he didn't want to be disturbed. Then I could tempt him with catnip mice, with strings and crumpled paper to no avail. Rabbit's time was his own, and he noticed us only when he chose to do so.

LLOYD ALEXANDER

The behavior of the cat, with or without man, has always been the most sagacious. There's no need to look any further for proof than its survival and its success in establishing itself in the hearts and minds of people, without giving much away or relinquishing its independence.

PAUL GALLICO

The naming of a cat, on the other hand, is something entirely else again. A cat who dislikes his name can, and I am reliably informed, often does, go through his entire lifetime without ever, even by a careless mistake, acknowledging that he has ever heard it before, let alone recognizing, in any perceptible manner known to humankind, that it could in any way have any possible connection with him.

CLEVELAND AMORY

Are cats lazy? Well, more power to them if they are. Which one of us has not entertained the dream of doing just as he likes, when and how he likes, and as much as he likes?

FERNAND MÉRY

Hark! She is calling to her cat.
She is down the misty garden in a tatter-brim straw hat,
And broken slippers grass-wet, treading tearful daisies.
But he does not heed her. He sits still and gazes.

RICHARD CHURCH

DIGNITY

But Cat said: "I am not a friend, and I am not a servant. I am the Cat who walks by himself, and all places are alike to me."

RUDYARD KIPLING

No favor can win gratitude from a cat.

JEAN DE LA FONTAINE

The cat does not, like the dog, depend entirely on human companionship; there are no touching stories of faithfulness to a departed master; there is no overwhelming interest in the human race. A cat has more of what the average Briton calls "self-respect," a quality he likes far better in himself than in others.

MARGARET BENSON

31

I love cats because I love my home, and little by little they become its visible soul. A kind of active silence emanates from these furry beasts who appear deaf to orders, to appeals, to reproaches and who move in a completely royal authority through the network of our acts, retaining only those which intrigue them or comfort them.

JEAN COCTEAU

DIGNITY

M. Fee, the naturalist, who has written so admirably about animals, and who understands, as only a Frenchman can understand, the delicate and subtle organization of a cat, frankly admits that the keynote of its character is independence. It dwells under our roofs, sleeps by our fire, endures our blandishments, and apparently enjoys our society, without for one moment forfeiting its sense of absolute freedom, without acknowledging any servile relation to the human creature who shelters it.

Rude and masterful souls resent this fine self-sufficiency in a domestic animal, and require that it shall have no will but theirs, no pleasure that does not emanate from them.

Yet there are people, less magisterial, perhaps, or less exacting, who believe that true friendship, even with an animal, may be built up on mutual esteem and independence; that to demand gratitude is to be unworthy of it; and that obedience is not essential to agreeable and healthy intercourse. A man who owns a dog is, in every sense of the word, its master; the term expresses accurately their mutual relations. But it is ridiculous when applied to the limited possession of a cat.

AGNES REPPLIER

Their Delightful
PLAYFULNESS

PLAYFULNESS

If encouraged, adult cats of all ages will play with people who love them. After the first playfulness of youth, some cats soon become meditative and grave; they seem to have a horror of useless movement. Yet when solicited by their masters, these same cats can rediscover all the liveliness of their salad days. They run after a ball, leap after a cork, roll about in mock fights, as if they had never outgrown their infancy—as if indeed, in relation to those humans in whom they had confidence, they always remained kittens.

FERNAND MÉRY

Their low tense bodies
   Like serpents pass,
And each imperceptible
   Smooth advance
Is an intricate step
   In a mystic dance,
Which ends in the cat
   From Number Three
Rushing quite suddenly
   Up a tree,

While mine walks off
   With a dignified air
To the other end
   Of Sycamore Square.
(But nobody yet
   Has ever found out
What in the world
   The game's about.)

JAN STRUTHER

PLAYFULNESS

Backward coil'd, and crouching low,
With glaring eye-balls watch thy foe,
The housewife's spindle whirling round,
Or thread, or straw, that on the ground
Its shadow throws, by urchin sly
Held out to lure thy roving eye;
Then, onward stealing, fiercely spring
Upon the futile, faithless thing.

JOANNA BAILLIE

...a dog for play needs a stimulating contact with someone else; that is already part of his sociable nature.

On the contrary, a cat also begins to play when you give her a stimulus; but she can play even if she is alone. She plays for her own self, in a solitary and individualistic way; you shut her up alone and a ball of wool, a fringe, or a dangling string are enough to start her off on a graceful and silent game.

KAREL CAPEK

It is the most irresistible comedian in the world. Its wide-open eyes gleam with wonder and mirth. It darts madly at nothing at all, and then, as though suddenly checked in the pursuit, prances sideways on its hind legs with ridiculous agility and zeal. It makes a vast pretence of climbing the rounds of a chair, and swings by the curtains like an acrobat.

AGNES REPPLIER

Their
CURIOSITY

CURIOSITY

Nothing is sacred to an exploring cat. Rabbit poked into closets and cupboards, crawled into the kitchen cabinets, and tested out the living room chairs. He caught sight of me closing a bureau drawer and immediately wanted it opened again, standing on his hind legs and trying to slip his paws into the crack. He examined my shirts, my wife's linen, and even took a nap in the drawer, just to get the feel of things.

LLOYD ALEXANDER

The kitten, accustomed to watch from the hotel home the dawn departure of climbers, decided one morning to follow in their footsteps. He was soon left behind, but after a long and lonely climb reached the Solway hut (12556 ft.). The next day he climbed still higher, and when night fell bivouacked in a couloir above the shoulder.

The next morning he was seen by a group of climbers, who passed him by, convinced that his climbing skill, if not his spirit, would be defeated by the difficult Ropes, Slabs and the Roof. They were wrong, and hours later the cat, miauing and tail up, reached the summit (14780 ft.), where the incredulous climbing party rewarded him with a share in their meal.

THE TIMES OF LONDON, SEPTEMBER 7, 1950

Their low tense bodies
 Like serpents pass,
And each imperceptible
 Smooth advance
Is an intricate step
 In a mystic dance,
Which ends in the cat
 From Number Three
Rushing quite suddenly
 Up a tree,
While mine walks off
 With a dignified air
To the other end
 Of Sycamore Square.
(But nobody yet
 Has ever found out
What in the world
 The game's about.)

JAN STRUTHER

An ordinary kitten will ask more questions than any five-year-old boy. He is the most catechismal of animals, with the possible exception of the monkey. Curiosity, indeed, is a predominant cat trait and a cat's first duty on entering a new domain is to explore every square inch of it. He not only examines every corner of the house he lives in but investigates the country for miles around.

CARL VAN VECHTEN

Their
CONFIDENCE
& EASE
in the World

CONFIDENCE & EASE

He never forgot his dignity. If he had asked to have the door opened, and was eager to go out, he always went deliberately; I can see him now, standing on the sill, looking about at the sky as if he was thinking whether it were worthwhile to take an umbrella, until he was near having his tail shut in.

CHARLES DUDLEY WARNER

CONFIDENCE & EASE

His amiable amber eyes
Are very friendly, very wise;
Like Buddha, grave and fat,
He sits, regardless of applause,
And thinking, as he kneads his paws,
What fun to be a cat!

CHRISTOPHER MORLEY

We are convinced that there is nothing in his being of which he is not at any moment totally aware, not only in its general appearance and color, grace, movement, or quality, but in its effect upon people or other animals, at any angle, against any background in innumerable emotional situations and states where he may be encountered. In short, we must say he knows that in his whole kingly person he is, as a wise friend once said about another of his like, ontologically perfect.

MARY TALLMOUNTAIN

Their Deep
MYSTERY

He entered the café. There was the cat, asleep. He ordered a cup of coffee, slowly stirred the sugar, sipped it (this pleasure had been denied him in the clinic), and thought, as he smoothed the cat's black coat, that this contact was an illusion and that the two beings, man and cat, were as good as separated by a glass, for man lives in time, in succession, while the magical animal lives in the present, in the eternity of the instant.

JORGE LUIS BORGES

The cat's drama is a drama of twilight, when the earth refreshed gives up her secret, subtle scents. Is it not to be played in broad daylight; it is a mystery play of things half revealed, subtly transformed, hardly understood, secretly suggestive.

MARGARET BENSON

Dear creature by the fire a-purr,
Strange idol, eminently bland,
Miraculous puss! As o'er your fur
I trail a negligible hand,

And gaze into your gazing eyes,
And wonder in a demi-dream,
What mystery it is that lies,
Behind those slits that glare and gleam.

LYTTON STRACHEY

MYSTERY

Cats are a mysterious kind of folk. There is more passing in their minds than we are aware of.

SIR WALTER SCOTT

Sphinx of my quiet hearth!
Thou deignst to dwell
Friend of my toil, companion of my ease,
Thine is the lore of Ra and Rameses;
That men forget thou dost remember well,
Beholden still in blinking reveries,
With sombre sea-green gaze inscrutable.

GRAHAM R. TOMSON

Their Silent and Intuitive
COMPANIONSHIP

Of all animals we can have in a room with us the cat is the least disquieting. Her presence is soothing to a student as the presence of a quiet nurse is soothing to an invalid. It is agreeable to feel that you are not absolutely alone, and it seems to you, when you are at work, as if the cat took care that all her movements should be noiseless, purely out of consideration for your comfort. Then, if you have time to caress her, you know that she will purr a response; and why doubt the sincerity of her affection?

PHILIP G. HAMERTON

Stately, kindly, lordly friend,
    Condescend
Here to sit by me, and turn
Glorious eyes that smile and burn,
Golden eyes, love's lustrous meed,
    On the golden page I read.

ALGERNON CHARLES SWINBURNE

Cats make one of the most satisfying sounds in the world: they purr. Almost all cats make us feel good about ourselves because they let us know they feel good about us, about themselves, and about our relationship with them. A purring cat is a form of high praise, like a gold star on a test paper. It is reinforcement for something we would all like to believe about ourselves—that we are nice.

ROGER A. CARAS

Sitting close to the fire, he seemed always interested in the conversation, and now and then, as he looked from one speaker to another, he would give a little protesting mew, as though in remonstrance to some opinion which he could not bring himself to share. He adored books and whenever he found one open on the table, he would sit down by it, look attentively at the printed page, turn over a leaf or two and finally fall asleep, for all the world as if he had been trying to read a modern novel. As soon as he saw me sit down to write, he would jump on my desk and watch the crooked and fantastic figures which my pen scattered over the paper, turning his head every time I began a fresh line. Sometimes it occurred to him to take a part in my work, and then he would make little clutches at my pen, with the evident design of writing a page or so…

THÉOPHILE GAUTIER

Is there anything more satisfying
on a cold, blustery day,
Than a good book,
A hearty fire,
And a soft purring friend by your side?

MARY MAUDE DANIELS

58

Cat and I lie breathless, drained,
curled around each other in front of the fire,
fur drying, bones melting into velvety cushions,
warmed, mesmerized by the flame dance.
The storm reverberates, vanquished,
in the distance. Snoring gently,
we are content.

NAN SHERMAN

It became obvious, in the following weeks, that Heathcliff was my personal cat. I could hardly go from one room to the next without having him follow me; if I left him on the bed or napping on his window sill and went elsewhere in the house, I would shortly hear a thump and a few moments later the big bushy cat would stalk up behind me. When I bent down to pat him, he rolled over gleefully—one of his favorite gestures of affection. Unlike Rabbit, he enjoyed being carried and let me pick him up willingly. He rested his enormous head on a spot just below my collarbone while his tail draped over my arm like an old blue shawl.

LLOYD ALEXANDER

I hesitate a little to speak of his capacity for friendship and the affectionateness of his nature, for I know from his own reserve that he would not care to have it much talked about. We understood each other perfectly, but we never made any fuss about it; when I spoke his name and snapped my fingers, he came to me; when I returned home at night, he was pretty sure to be waiting for me near the gate, and would rise and saunter along the walk, as if his being there were purely accident, so shy was he commonly of showing feeling.

CHARLES DUDLEY WARNER

The Wisdom and
PEACEFULNESS
of Older Cats

He blinks upon the hearthrug,
And yawns in deep content,
Accepting all the comforts
That Providence has sent.

Loud he purrs and louder,
In one glad hymn of praise
For all the night's adventures,
For quiet restful days.

Life will go on forever,
With all that cat can wish,
Warmth and the glad procession
Of fish and milk and fish.

Only — the thought disturbs him —
He's noticed once or twice,
The times are somehow breeding
A nimbler breed of mice.

ALEXANDER GRAY

Those who love cats which do not even purr,
Or which are thin and tired and very old,
Bend down to them in the street and stroke their fur
And rub their ears and smooth their breast, and hold
Their paws, and gaze into their eyes of gold.

FRANCIS SCARFE

PEACEFULNESS

No more frisking as of old,
Or chasing his shadow over the lawn,
But a dignified old person, tickling
His nose against twig or flower in the border,
Until evening falls and bed-time's in order,
Unable to keep eyes open any longer
He waits for me to carry him upstairs
To nestle all night snug at foot of bed—
My cat and I grow old together.

A.L. ROWSE

PICTURE CREDITS

PICTURE CREDITS

34   Oliver Herford. The Kitten's Garden of Verses, 1911.

35   Henriette Ronner-Knip. The School of Painters, c. 1890.

36   John William Godward. The Favourite, 1901.

37   top: Janusz Grabianski. From *Cats*, 1966.   bottom: Unknown. From *The Animal Object Book*, c. 1890.

38   Janusz Grabianski. From Cats, 1966.

39   Jessie Willcox Smith. Magazine cover, 1932.

40   Henriette Ronner-Knip. Artful Play.

41   Anne Anderson and Alan Wright. From *The Nursery Zoo,* c. 1918.

42   E. Morley. The Trespassers.

43   Nicholas Tarkhoff. Two Children With a Cat on a Window Ledge.

44   top: Unknown. From *Robin's Christmas Song*.   bottom: Frank Paton. Who's the Fairest of Them All?, 1883.

45   Muriel Dawson. From *Mother Goose,* 1940.

46   Unknown. Book illustration.

47   top: Unknown. Postcard.   bottom: Sei Koyanagui. Cat On a Rush Chair.

48   top: Stark Davis. Magazine cover, 1931.   bottom: L.H. Jungnickel. Liegende Katze.

49   top: Louis Wain. Painting.   bottom: Unknown. Lydia and Tabitha, c. 1830.

50   Henri Rousseau. Portrait of Pierre Loti, detail, 1891.

51   Henrietta Shore. My Cat, c. 1930.

52   top: Fernando Botero. The Cat.   bottom: Tian Yuan. From *Chinese Folk Toys and Ornaments,* 1980.

53   top: Ernst Ludwig Kirchner. Grey Cat on a Cushion, 1919.   bottom: Unknown. Scrap.

54   Wladimir Sutejew. From *Lustige Geschichten.*

55   top: Pierre-Auguste Renoir. Portrait of Julie Manet, 1887.

        bottom: Pierre-Auguste Renoir. Sleeping Girl with Cat, 1880.

56   Arthur Rackham. Book illustration, c. 1900.

57   top: Cecilia Beaux. Sita and Sarita.   bottom: Jan Cornelisz Vermeyen. The Holy Family, detail, c. 1500.

58   top: Clara M. Burd. Magazine cover, 1911.   bottom: Auguste Renoir. Woman With a Cat, 1875.

59   top: H. Guerault. Reclining Lady With a Cat.   bottom: Marcus Stone. Good Friends, 1887.

60   top: Emile Munier. A Special Moment, 1874.   bottom: Marcus Stone. The End of the Story.

61   top: Helen Sewell. From *Bluebonnets for Lucinda,* 1934.   bottom: Julian Alden Wier. Little Lizzie Lynch.

62   Charles Le Brun. The Sleep of the Infant Jesus, detail, 1655.

63   Unknown Japanese watercolor, c. 1950.

64   Carl Holsøe. A Saucer of Milk.

65   Antonio Rotta. The Old Lady and Her Cat, 1880.

68   Mary Baker. From The Black Cat and the Tinker's Wife, 1926.

Back Cover   Mary Baker. From The Black Cat and the Tinker's Wife, 1926.